"This book is a lit... ... pages a beautiful reminder to step out of the fast-forward lives we lead, and bathe in the silent wisdom that lies within. The very essence of the mystical way, and a truth found at the heart of all the world's great wisdom traditions, it is that for which we all yearn."

John Greer, SeeingKnowingBeing

"Jim Young takes the spiritual pilgrim on a twenty-first century journey into the world of life purpose—he challenges the seeker to look within, not beyond, for the road map."

Jenny Wagget, The Awakening Dream

"Jim Young's truth is profound; his ability to so succinctly communicate it is genius. Open the door to the truth, peace and fulfillment within you now."

James C. Wilhelm, I Am God and So Are You

"A much-needed and insightful exploration of finding our inner strength and contributing it to the world."

Annie Woods, Journeys to Places Out of Bounds

Published in collaboration with creationspirit.net

ISBN-13: 978-1519473233; 1519473230

PREFACE

On any given day, a dizzying array of media platforms bombards us with messaging promising us a healthier body, a better social life, a highly successful business, an endless array of friends, and on it goes. All we need do is invest in sculpting ourselves into a "new and improved" version, focusing on some aspect of our bodies, lives, careers, or relationships we currently consider less than good enough. Join the 21-day meditation program! Sign up for our magical physical fitness class! Try the Paleo diet! Find a guru! The list of self-improvement opportunities is endless, as are their promises of becoming better in some way.

Before you succumb to the blaring deadlines counting down the "deep discounts" on this course or that, how about finding out who you really are and what truly makes you happy? Rather than changing your wardrobe or following someone else's formula, try first connecting to your true inner Voice, the same voice you've been drowning out as you chase a concept or idea of success and fulfillment that may not even be yours. This isn't "that little voice in your head" that's constantly judging everyone and everything you do. This is the voice that connects you with your innate state of being in a way that serves to guide you in being true to your Self. This is the voice that affirms your spiritual reality and replaces the ego consciousness that insists we aren't "good enough" to be accepted by our friends and loved ones, or even ourselves.

In less time each day than it takes to meditate, jog, to take a walk in nature, or even fix a healthy breakfast, you can connect to that undeniable inner source that affirms:

- you already are what you seek;
- you are complete in the ways that truly count;
- you are the ineffable essence called love;
- the truth of your purpose is found within *you*, rather than

from some external
authority.

If you're ready to live anew, to be
free from erroneous or harmful
beliefs and opinions, and to have a
profound inner guide readily
available to you at any time of day or
night, read on. And as you do, listen
carefully for what resonates as Truth
for you. Then simply follow what
you receive by asking yourself the
Three Questions each day. Many
have already begun. Their lives have
changed in ways unimaginable. Dare
to join them, walking your own
walk, fulfilling your life's purpose
with enthusiasm.

Are you ready? Okay, let's begin.

Namasté! I honor as divine
you and all life on this planet.
With this declaration, I'm not
honoring the divine *in* you; I
honor *you* as a completely
divine being. As are we all.

My purpose is sharing how the Three
Questions can empower you to free
yourself from opinions and beliefs

learned from others and to live in resonance with what you will come to know as *your* Truth. That, indeed, you are divine and sacred, as are all living things on Earth.

If you're like most people, you probably struggle mightily to achieve success by whatever definition you have chosen, which may in fact be someone else's. You work hard, keep your nose to the grindstone, and never give up because you've been taught we need to struggle in order to survive. In fact, we're all so busy performing a script someone else wrote, or living up to others' expectations of us, that we're no longer sure we're living by our *own* definition of success. Or even know our true identity.

Misidentification is a real barrier in our lives. Most of us identify ourselves by the roles we play, or by how someone else has identified us: parent, lover, doctor, teacher, child… on it goes, endlessly.

Let me tell you a story. The story is about a group of people who gathered for refreshments at the close of a seminar one evening. The conversation turned to the ethnicity and nationality of Jesus. People suggested all manner of "evidence":

Jesus had to be Mexican because -

1. His name was Jesus. (pronounced hay-zuss)
2. He was bilingual.
3. He was always being harassed by the authorities.

But others put forth the equally valid arguments that:

Jesus was a person of color because -

1. He called everyone "brother."
2. He liked Gospel.
3. He couldn't get a fair trial.

Jesus was Italian because -

1. He talked with his hands.

2. He had wine with every meal.
3. He used olive oil.

And still another that:

Jesus was Californian because -

1. He never cut his hair.
2. He walked around barefoot.
3. He started a new religion.

Others crowded the debate with equally solid arguments:

Jesus was Irish because -

1. He never got married.
2. He was always telling stories.
3. He loved green pastures.

and even that Jesus was a woman because -

1. She fed a crowd at a moment's notice.
2. Men didn't understand her.
3. Even when dead, she

arose to complete her work.

But perhaps the most compelling evidence of all was:

Jesus was Jewish because -

1. He went into his father's business.
2. He lived at home until he was 33.
3. He was sure his mother was a virgin, and his mother was sure he was God.

I couldn't possibly guess where this anecdote might have taken you just now, but I hope you have at least enjoyed it. My intent was to raise the issue of identification—or to be more specific, misidentification.

I would posit that perhaps the thickest wall standing between what or who we think we are and our inner reality—our spiritual identity—is that we have no idea how immense the potential of our purpose, creativity and demonstration is. So many of us misidentify ourselves by the endless roles we play, thinking they are what defines our identity. And depending on how well we fulfill those roles, we often end up declaring that we're simply not "good enough." After all, if we were good enough, why wouldn't our prayers have been answered? Why are we not successful in the eyes of others, not to say ourselves? Why do some of our relationships go astray?

Our misrepresentation of what we are stems primarily from seeing ourselves as so small, so insignificant, that we act precisely that way—as not even "good enough." It's a self-fulfilling prophecy. We then use that lens of "not good enough" to view our life and our role in it, and that causes us to attract circumstances, people, and experiences that validate and deepen our sense of smallness. In other words, when we forget how powerful and influential we truly are, we behave accordingly.

This book is about opening up a new, vibrant view of life, about adopting an attitude and philosophy that expand our worldview well beyond the limitations with which we've shackled ourselves. It's about acknowledging and being continuously aware that we are ^very the embodiment of potential. That our identity lies within the truth of what we truly are, not who others have led us to believe we are.

You can think of the Three Questions as a tool to help us validate our real identity. When these questions are practiced faithfully, our spiritual identity takes on absolute clarity, and we begin to live as the divine beings we already are.

It may be tempting to try and reason or think your way through this book. Resist that temptation. Instead, try dropping your focus about a foot lower, into your heart of hearts, the only place where the truth of your being resides. Where you can be guided moment to moment with pinpoint accuracy—not only about what you are but your relationship with your highest self, your innate being.

This book is about letting go of all those conditioned beliefs and opinions about success and living true to your self. Life is not, and should not be, about struggling. Life is about getting out of our own way so life's gifts can come to us. Spiritually speaking, nothing else matters.

The answers you'll gain from the Three Questions process are about a very different thing: the nature of your relationship with your deepest Self, the highest version of yourself—and in this never-ending inward awareness to fully comprehend that you *are far more* immense that you give yourself credit for.

As you practice the Three Questions, you'll see that you already hold within all you need to live your life's purpose at the deepest levels of being. This is your life, and only you can create it. Only you are in charge of it. Only you can be it.

This process will develop your ability to be aware of and reveal the never-ending gifts of your inner Voice. It will build your confidence in being true to yourself—the real gift of life that foments your success, no matter what others may tell you life is about or how you should live it.

In my workshops where I teach the Three Questions, I like to give participants a meaningful foundation for spiritual renewal. But because we all learn differently, and may find ourselves at different points on the spiritual path, you are always free to learn in the ways that most effectively engage you. Perhaps you already feel free to engage in new ways of being (i.e., you are "aware"). If so, you may be tempted to go directly to **Chapter Nine, "The Way,"** which initiates the process of the Three Questions.

Whatever your personal approach may be to the Three Questions, I do encourage you at the very least to skim the other chapters to reinforce the foundation that is so vital to mastering this process. You might have a new insight, or see something you already know in a different light, a fresh perspective. If anything "ignites your heart," feel free to use it until and unless you hear a finer version in your own heart of hearts, as your *own* way in the world.

Whichever way you choose to begin this empowering process, YOU GOT THIS! Of that you can be sure. Ask. Listen. Trust.

I do not really give you new
commands.
I have so few to give.
Only I tell them in different
ways, so as you teach others
you can reach people with
common needs
but who need to hear
about them
in different ways.

Jim Young, from *AS IF
FROM GOD,*

Chapter 1
The Context

Some would argue that what you are about to engage and master is but another way to pray—a significantly different way.

Organized religion teaches us many ways to pray. Most religions misrepresent the very intent and purpose of prayer that has been passed down to us by sages and poets throughout history. These sages, mystics, and poets have been admonishing us to obtain direction for living spiritually by going inward, closeted in the stillness of our deepest self, with the doors (to belief, opinion, and ego consciousness) closed, so that in stillness and silence we could hear our Voice, the voice of Truth within each of us.

Yet, in most religious settings, we're taught to pray out loud, together, as one, as believers in the same prayer we're told is proper for us.

Sadly, the following quip illustrates the miscasting of prayer:

"Give someone a fish and they'll eat for a day; give them religion and they'll starve to death while praying for a fish."

Jesus, among others, defined prayer in a way that the dominant religious authorities of his time considered subversive, threatening tradition and ritual. Indeed, if we were to follow his inward reckoning faithfully, we would find ourselves praying unceasingly, the result of simply *listening* for the Awareness.

When we faithfully trust and follow what we know to be True to that inner Voice, the guidance we receive is fulfilled, without question or doubt. Turning to this inward Voice that speaks in silence virtually "guarantees" that all of our prayers will be fulfilled successfully—skepticism and doubt aside—simply by realigning our definition and demonstration of prayer.

Before we go into what I call the "Inward Journey," which naturally engages prayer as I have come to understand how Jesus meant it—listening in the depths of your heart—let's take a moment to contemplate the meaning of living spiritually.

Why, you may ask, do we need to consider a concept that so many of us already know? Because, the sages of old have told us that in order to know God, we need to understand that we can know God only spiritually, inwardly. * "The Kingdom of God is within you," for example. (Luke: 14-21). So, if we're even thinking of praying *to* something we call God, we might well benefit from having a spiritual context for doing so.

Also, because we're so accustomed to looking outward for answers to our questions, for life's direction, we will need to take a decidedly different path to gain that deeper insight and guidance we seek: reliance on our own highest form of self.

What we need is a way to receive, at all times, the intuitions, insights, and information we want or need. It's like having an "inner Google" to serve our every need.

By "spiritual" I mean the process of turning inward to whatever it is we call the ineffable wisdom that speaks to what we really are. We are infinitely more capable, talented, intelligent, and intuitive than we allow ourselves to believe, and it is this immensity that we call God. In reality, it is our own infinite potential waiting but to be heard. To be trusted. To be followed.

* See Chapter Five for a discussion about the concept of "God."

Chapter 2
The Spirituality Pre-test

Let's take a spiritual pre-test of sorts, which will clarify your relationship with your inner Voice, when your mind is quiet enough so you can truly hear. For each of the statements that follow, simply respond with a yes or no:

I live without caffeine or nicotine;

I am able to feel cheerful and ignore aches and pains;

I'm able to resist complaining;

I understand when loved ones are too busy for me;

I can take criticism and blame without resentment;

I can resist the temptation to correct others if I know more about a particular subject;

I treat the rich and poor alike;

I'm able to face the world without lies or deceit;

I can conquer most forms of stress without medical help;

I harbor no prejudice against creed, color, religion, gender, sexual preference, or politics.

Okay, then, if you have mastered all of these, you have reached the same level of spiritual development as—your pet dog.

I jest, of course. But living spiritually is not a laughing matter. In large part, living spiritually is about not taking yourself too seriously and realizing that most of what we do and say in this realm is repeating the ideas and concepts of others, thinking them to be our own.

It is this form of humility that affirms the real source of meaning is found within, that we feel safe enough to listen inwardly for the quiet but significant Voice that brings us real knowing and insight.

Chapter 3
Defining Spirituality

Living spiritually refers to focusing wholly and completely on our inner Voice, and to faithfully follow the insights and intuitions we receive, demonstrating what we discern there. In plain language, we could say this means living true to yourself.

Unfortunately, our lifelong adherence to the voice of ego consciousness in our heads has us thinking that all we really need for living successfully we can find without rather than within. This statement came from my inner Voice a few years ago—a clear, if not earth-shattering, message that brought this illusion into sharp focus: "We pray, we meditate, we do yoga, we fast, we become vegans, we seek, we study, we live in an ashram and worship yogis. Ego needs all kinds of fuel." These are certainly all fine things to invest our energy in; and yet, in and of themselves, they aren't spiritual. They can only lead us to the deeper spiritual path we seek.

Your ego may resist the ironic truth of this comment; and if it does, use that discomfort to lead you to your inner Truth.

A rather apt message from Deepak Chopra, circulated on social media, showed up on Facebook a short time ago and tells us: "Religion is belief in someone else's experience. Spirituality is having your own experience."

Or, another: "Religion is crowd control; spirituality is our personal relationship with our divinity." (Author unknown)

Given this context, spirituality is not about religion, acting piously, what we eat, or whom we admire or hang around with. Spirituality is about accessing and activating cosmic, spiritual inner consciousness. It begins by communing with inner awareness, and is activated by exercising trust in what we have discerned as the truth of our spiritual journey through trust in outward demonstration.

Working through this process is like taking in the breath of life. Exercising or extending that inner knowing into the world is the "out breath" of life, the extension of Love outward to others. In this way, the gift and giving become One. This is what forms spiritual creation, what epitomizes spiritual relationships.

Whenever you hear or read anything of a spiritual nature that moves you deep within—touches your soul— you are not learning something new. You are remembering what you have always known on a deeper level. It is but a gentle awakening, a simple reminder of what resonates with your fundamental nature.

I'll never forget the moment I realized that the purpose of having released 16 books into the world was not about writing and publishing books, but about learning to listen inwardly. At that instant, this penetrating message of my life's purpose and the importance of prayer, of listening inwardly, was etched indelibly into my heart and soul.

Indeed, my inner Voice had spoken loud and clear. It called to share a simple process that could work for anyone, despite any beliefs, opinions and religious upbringing.

Chapter 4
Our Spiritual Vision

Prayer has a profound personal meaning for each one of us; it's important to fully grasp that meaning if we are to fully release its power.

We're all together on this spiritual journey continuum, albeit in different places—so be careful not to throw out your own unique relationship to prayer with the bath water. However you define prayer and however you pray, it's perfectly valid for where you are now. No one place or time is better than another, necessarily; each simply represents a position along your continuum, without judgment or obligation.

I heard one of the most pragmatic definitions of prayer during a mass at the Newman Center in Potsdam, New York, in the late 1970s. The late Father Bernie Kellogg, celebrant at that occasion, amusingly summarized the week's spiritual accomplishments for the students in his congregation, concluding with these words: "Oh, mighty God, now for some good news. Surely you have noticed that there was an huge increase in prayers this week from all these bright college students—and by that you know it must be exam week!"

Levity aside, we can access the deeper layers of meaning that prayer carries, or holds as potential, in a surprisingly simple way. And that is, accepting and knowing that you already have the source of prayer within you—that it's really just awaiting your awareness.

In other words, prayer naturally expresses what we really are—the divine, ineffable essence of being, extended through *all* we do. This is tantamount to making or expressing love all day, in every way possible. In one form or another, we express either love or fear. Simple awareness of one or the other will tell us clearly what we are sending out into the Universe.

Ego consciousness would have us think we have limitless choices we can make in answer to our prayers, implanting the erroneous definition of free will into our psyche. When we come to fully comprehend the empowering nature of our innate spiritual awareness, it becomes abundantly clear that there really is no alternative to the inner Voice.

It is this clarity, this spiritual assurance, that makes us aware that "free will" simply means that following or willing the Truth of our being that is heard only inwardly is what frees us from erroneously following the Ego. Thus the erroneous idea of "free will" becomes the spiritual reality of "freeing the will," or following our true will freely—unencumbered or unrestrained by outside influence or the pitfalls of ego consciousness.

The ego determines its actions largely according to perceived neediness and separation, and molds our behavior to fit a false image of prayer. By going within, we gain the spiritual clarity we need to guide our external behavior.

Living through ego consciousness produces a life that is largely chaotic and misleading, and generally provides ill-defined means for living spiritually. Living from the inside out, on the other hand, we get in touch with our innate purpose and come to trust it for our life's direction.

When engaged in prayer based on ego consciousness, we inevitably end up asking why our prayers are not always answered. Why is it when we pray, not for us but for someone else, say a loved one's recovery from illness, they may not necessarily get better? Why it is that so often when we pray to heal a relationship, it breaks up instead? Why do we pray for life when we all have bodies that shall die someday?

The list of prayers and unanswered entreaties goes on and on, and yet we continue to follow this means of praying, believing that all we need do is love God more and more, be a better and better person, and (perhaps) someone or something "out there" will finally answer our prayers, just in the way we want them answered. Surrendering to such *make* admonitions is to making someone or something we think of as God an idol in *our own* image and likeness.

Surely, we can go deeper to find what we innately know is the truth about prayer. But where and how do we reach this depth? Sages have often told us that the only place to find deeper meaning is by going inward, clearing out our mental distractions and listening in the depth of our heart for moment-by-moment direction for our lives. Truly, our only imperative is to listen inwardly, where wisdom and inspiration await. Unfortunately, we've been taught by various religious leaders to follow their authority in how we live, so much so that that practice has become habit. On the other hand, as we grow spiritually, we find that our only imperative is to listen inwardly, to our innate Voice of wisdom and inspiration.

But what is this voice we hear? Is it the voice of something separate from us, which we call God and which has only our individual good in mind for us? It would seem so. But the reality might not be so easy. Perhaps we could benefit from coming to grips with what we have been calling 'God'.

Chapter 5
Who or What is This One to Whom We Pray?

I'm glad you asked. Try this one on for size: that which we call 'God' is the wholeness of creative genius, the potential of cosmic intelligence waiting for awareness and demonstration. God is all that is, and infinitely so; God is the innate meaning and definition of eternal life. In this sense, God is pure omnipresence: everyone, everything, everywhere.

In this spiritual view, we are *also* God individually expressed, as are all living things, trees, and vegetation—indeed, *all* of life. Every element and every aspect of our planet and the known universe are the full expression of spiritual consciousness, just waiting to be realized.

This supreme, all-encompassing consciousness pervades the Universe and gives order to life. It contains in its wholeness all that is necessary for its manifestation into life's multitude of expressions. All it takes for it to manifest is for us to honor our awareness and acknowledgement of it as the source of our being—and our willingness to accept, trust, and demonstrate it into being.

Such is the gift of inner awareness expressed perpetually, infinitely. Just remember that our relationship with the outside world begins in our relationship with our inner source. Thus is prayer heard and thus it materializes into reality.

This explanation of "God" may seem rather unusual, to say the least. Yet, as we come to understand that we are not our body, but rather the demonstration of divine essence of being through all we do, we begin to behave as though we—each one of us—are God. Not a god or the god, simply God. This is contrary to behaving like we're not divine simply because we have forgotten that we are. Or by virtually chaining ourselves to the illusions of ego consciousness, refusing to acknowledge our innate state of being.

Our lives and our identity are continually expressed as the essence of life (some would call it Love) through all we do. Truly, what we are, and the prayers we bring to life, are expressions of wisdom, inspiration, insight, enlightenment, our innate fiber of spiritual being by whatever name—the voice of wholeness, one single, holy relationship.

To express our nature otherwise is to live by exterior signs and symbols, the illusory entrapment that accompanies the dictates of ego consciousness, the voice of separation and difference. Ego consciousness requires separation and difference in order to continue the illusion that we are our body.

To be sure, whatever viewpoint we base our lives on becomes the life we see around us. It becomes the *how* in our experience of life. As creators of our life, we use our trowel or brush to paint a landscape that represents either ego consciousness or spiritual consciousness. A world either of chaos, ignorance, confusion and doubt fueled by fear—or a world lovingly experienced through peace, joy, reverence for the dignity of life and fulfillment of our innate being as loving energy personified. The truth of our being becomes our song to be sung, to be fully lived, experienced each in our own unique expressions of the divine.

Walt Whitman spoke of wisdom this way: "Now I will do nothing but listen, to accrue what I hear into this song." What a masterful message of living true to our inner Voice this is! Even further, the poetic admonition to *be* that very song each moment of our lives touches us deeply, reverently.

Jesus, among others, gave us the means of discerning, of defining prayer for each of us, by going inward and listening for the infinite Voice—our very own innate Voice—as the Voice of prayer to be fulfilled. This sounds simple, but can it be exercised simply?

Chapter 6
Going Inward

To begin with, we can practice hearing our inner Voice, which is what some would call being inspired or becoming enlightened.

For example, instead of seeking answers outside ourselves from experts and authorities of all kinds, we can simply inquire of ourselves. To know and accept that we really do not know, in the ego-intellect, is to free ourselves from seeking those external answers. It's then that we finally understand the direction and clarification we seek lie within. We learn to experience truth by asking only where truth *can* be heard: *within*.

The contemplative monk, Thomas Keating, admonished us: "Silence is the language God speaks. All the rest is nothing but a bad mistranslation."

Many, though, seem fearful—at the very least, reluctant—to learn what resides within. Do we really know what's in our hearts? Do we really want to know? Or does the fear that lurks inside hold us back?

For the past several years, a story has been making the rounds that speaks to our seeming unwillingness to seek the truth of our being—at least inwardly. The story goes like this:

> Once there was a man walking down a street at night, and he came upon another man under a street-lamp, on all fours, searching through the grass clearly looking for something.
>
> "What are you looking for?" asked the man.
>
> "I'm looking for my keys—I've lost my keys. That's my house over there, and I've lost my keys."

"May I help you look?"

So both men got down on all fours. They searched and they searched and at last the man who'd come along said, "Are you sure you lost your keys here?"

The man said, "No, they're not lost here. They're in the house."

"Then why aren't we looking for them in the house?"

"Because it's dark in my house."

Indeed, it's dark in our inner house, where we closet the truth, the truth than can be heard only within. At least that's what many of us fear: the boogieman hiding in the dark, in whatever form he might take. So, many—most, I suspect—look outward, mostly to others, for the root and cause of their decisions, perhaps fearful of making a mistake, or even of being right.

For example, when couples dine out together, you can often witness one spouse asking the other what they're interested in before they order for themselves. To make matters worse, it often turns out that if one orders something different from the other, it isn't too long before he or she regrets his/her own decision: "Oh, gee, I wish I ordered what you did."

Our "real" body, the infinite, ineffable source of our being, will never lie to us, yet we often rely on external authorities for guidance— until we discern how futile that is.

At best, all we can get from others is what may have worked for them at one time or another. But that doesn't necessarily mean what worked for them is right for us. Why would we want to put their head on our shoulders? Seeking the answers within is "the way" for each of us.

It is said that Jesus told us that he was "The Way," "The Inward Journey." What he really meant by this is that "The Way" refers to *how* he lived his life—from the inside out. This is the living example we should also follow, the path that faithfully discloses our unique inner truth.

"The Way" is not a path outside of us. "The Way" *is* us. It is who and what we are, without influence or alteration from the outside.

A Native American medicine man in rural New Mexico once said, "The path to God is seven billion lanes wide, and growing." As divine beings and expressions of All That Is, we *all* are the way, individually and uniquely expressed, but not separate from the wholeness of spiritual reality. We are all this very same 'I Am.'" Thus, his description of how to pray becomes the definition of his way—and thus, our very own. And it forms our very identity.

The following chapters give you one means of building confidence in this way of prayer, the very same way Jesus ordered his life by going within to seek his truth. It's the way that breathes life into our being—which not only creates our identity, but leads others by example to do likewise. Our relationship with prayer, our relationship with our very own inner Voice, is exemplified through its common expression within us and with others. Such acknowledgment, trust, and manifestation define the divine relationship.

Chapter 7
Added Validation

No matter what our religious or spiritual background, we sometimes want affirmation that it's safe to consider an alternative. For example, it was Mother Teresa who said, "God speaks in the silence of the heart. Listening is the beginning of prayer."

Psalms, 46:10 gives us "Be still and know I am God."

And from Jesus himself: "Go inward in secret, close the door and listen."

What all three quotes refer to is not an exercise of the mind, but rather one of experiencing one's own innate wisdom or enlightened being, which extends out into the Universe as the ultimate form of love—living true to our Self in all circumstances and conditions. Yet, if we don't go inward, how will we ever find the gems that await us?

A few more references follow, some accompanied by my personal comments.

Proverbs 3:5&6
"Trust in the Lord (law of order/truth begets truth), with all thy heart; lean not unto your own understanding (intellect, literal, outer signs, beliefs and opinions). In all thy ways acknowledge Him (Wisdom) and He (Wisdom) shall direct your paths."

Mahatma Gandhi
"Prayer is not asking. It is a longing of the soul. It is daily admission of one's weakness. It is better in prayer to have a heart without words than words without a heart."

Psalm 91
"He that dwelleth in the secret place of the most high shall abide under the shadow (hidden enlightenment that frees the shadow) of the almighty."

Saint Teresa of Avila
"Prayer is nothing else than being on terms of friendship with God."

John 15

"If ye abide in me (the Christ, wisdom, divine/spiritual consciousness), and my words abide in you (your awareness of symbolic meaning, inspiration), it shall be done unto you (you activate inspiration into Being).

Sören Kierkegaard
"Just as in earthly life lovers long for the moment when they are able to breathe forth their love for each other, to let their souls blend in a soft whisper, so the mystic longs for the moment when in prayer he can, as it were, creep into God."

I Samuel 3:9
"Speak Lord, thy servant heareth."
"Fear not, it is I, God," "Be still and know I am God."

Adam Clarke
"Prayer requires more of the heart than of the tongue."

John 18:36
"My kingdom is not of this world."
We don't really experience anything in the physical world. We experience it inwardly as resonance with divine

consciousness—or not. Otherwise, we have ears and do not hear, eyes and do not see.

William Ralph Inge
"Prayer gives a man the opportunity of getting to know a gentleman he hardly ever meets. I do not mean his maker, but himself."

Marianne Williamson
"I think of prayer as a lifeline back to where I most want to be."

Victor Hugo
"Prayer is an august avowal of ignorance."

Eckhart Tolle
"I am praying to my self for guidance—to the true self that sees things as they are without the overlay of various hopes and fears. It recognizes when I have become caught in the ego's way of thinking, and is ever-willing to help set me free."

Wayne Dyer
"Everything coming from Source is on purpose. Be thankful while

empowering your reconnection to that form from which you and everything else originated."

Rumi
"There is a voice that doesn't use words... Listen!"

To summarize, surrendering to the inner Voice fulfills the experience of the same. Surrender is not a capitulation to some outer influence, a caving-in out of fear. It's aligning our presence with the full awareness of our own inner wisdom. When fully aware, we surrender to this innate communion with grace, the tongue that speaks only our Truth to be expressed.

It is the full acknowledgment of the power of our innate wisdom in our lives that becomes our reality—giving no power to outer authority whatsoever. This is our true identity, our true character speaking to us. That's the hand we hold as we go along on our spiritual journey.

Chapter 8
Redefining Prayer

It may sound strange to you, but we are whole and perfect—always have been, always will be. So what's to pray for?

Quite simply, prayer is communion. It's our relationship with inward awareness. The late Yogi Bhajan, spiritual leader of the Sikh community, said, "If you can't see God *in* all, you can't see God *at* all." I would suggest we take this one step further. Not to see God *in* someone or some thing, but rather to see all *as* God personified. And yet, in desperation (usually out of fear), we manufacture some outer God or idol to take care of things, to change things for us.

Just think for a moment about what our world would be like if God—the spiritual reality of God—was *everything* to us. *Nothing* would trouble us!

I've often wondered: Why don't we always receive the answers we want to what we call prayer? In some ways, it's because we come to prayer with erroneous expectations. God is not Santa Claus. God, as we have defined the concept in this book, can be seen as Wisdom seeking our awareness and demonstration through inspiration. Therefore, it's only within that we find what we normally seek without.

Want peace? Be the peace you seek. Want happiness? Be happy. Want prosperity? Go within to the source of inspiration, which provides true prosperity. Want divine relationships that bring out the divine in both parties? Be one. Want success? Go within for perpetual guidance, not just once but step by step—and follow it through to the end.

But be forewarned: your ideas of success, wealth, and happiness are likely to change along the way as what you had thought or hoped might fulfill you is gradually—or perhaps more suddenly—replaced by a deeper awareness, a larger view of your self and thus your world.

Prayer is not about getting something or changing something; it's about being true to what we *already are*. It's the inner Voice that tells us what we seek already *is*—and thus what is to be. So *be* it! We're human *beings*, after all, not human *doings*. As such, being, "isness," is our business! Prayer becomes an act of experiencing and following God (wisdom), not fear, as our true purpose. Indeed, this is the definition of living artfully: "isness" as usual.

"The Way," of which sages and poets have spoken for millennia, is the built-in mechanism for initiating and perpetuating spiritual transformation and transcendence. "The Way," the journey inward, is about becoming aware of, trusting and demonstrating our own deific nature. *We* are the prayer being witnessed. Inspiration and intuition embody the spiritual consciousness that becomes our way of being.

How do we go inward? It's about deciding, consciously, to gain awareness by listening within rather than without. It's not about all that

noise we make when we pray—
continually asking some illusory god
or external idol to bail us or a friend
out, or the fear, the doubt, the "what
ifs" that keep truth from witnessing
itself. As we open our heart, we
become more receptive to reflections
of truth.

In a way, we're much like the tuner
in a radio; and the static is akin to the
distractions of our monkey mind that
make it impossible to hear the pure
frequencies, to tune in with clarity.
We need to identify and create a new
habit—a habit of listening, which is
what the "Inward Journey" is all
about.

Listening inwardly emanates from an
attitude—and general approach to
life—of wonder and awe. We
become and stay aware of inner
wisdom and inspiration, and come to
love them with all our mind, heart,
and strength. These qualities are
forever renewing themselves and us
with them. This is what defines
unceasing prayer.

A Course In Miracles tells us the purpose of prayer as most of us practice it is to escape from some form of fear. That is to say, the underlying need for a specific prayer stems from a desire to free ourselves from whatever we fear in the *outer world*—death, bodily harm, injury, lack, abandonment, and so on. Thus prayer and freedom from fear have the same purpose: to return to the perfection that we already *are*.

The answers to our prayers, as they are heard and experienced, transcend the physical body. They are sudden shifts (intuition, insight, enlightenment) in the body of cosmic consciousness, away from the focus on the material, physical aspects of our reality that ego consciousness perpetuates. That is how the inner Voice cleanses our consciousness of fear, the very fear that previously clouded these answers from our view.

This kind of inner discernment induces a state in which fear simply cannot exist. Thus prayers are a means and end, all in one. And, like miracles, no prayer is more or less important than any other. A prayer is simply an inspiration brought to life.

The answers we find in and through prayer are expressions of love and wisdom, although they do not always have observable effects. This may be why we're often unsure whether our prayers have been "answered"— because we're so accustomed to looking for the physical, material, observable change. The only real change lies in spiritual awareness.

What we're really looking for, through prayer, is atonement. I call this *at-one-ment*, where we conceive of our material life experience and inner wisdom as one. Until we achieve this at-one-ment, we cannot expect to access our own divine order, that is, the guidance that is best for us as individual human beings.

Prayer helps to correct and redirect misperception regardless of the degree or kind of what I call *spiritual error* (fear, ego, or any other thought or emotion that leads us astray from our true path). It is truly indiscriminating. Prayer identifies what is in accord with truth (wisdom) as true, and rejects what is out of accord with it as false. In other words, when we understand the purpose and nature of prayer and uncouple it from our ego, we no longer pray for the wrong things.

Prayer is our inner process that tells us how and where we should invest our full trust and faith. This is the alchemy, the trust and awareness that transform reliance on ego consciousness into reliance on inspirational reality—changing belief in ego consciousness into inner heart awareness.

It's listening inwardly, allowing the Voice heard only in silence to speak, that represents exercising our inner feminine. When we adhere to the direction and purpose of what is heard there, when we put it into practice, this corresponds to exercising our inner masculine. This is meant in a spiritual rather than societal context, for such designations are not based on gender, but on the relative purpose of each: feminine, to receive, accept; masculine, to put into action, to faithfully abide.

When we practice going inward to access our purpose and our path, faithfully, day in and day out, we are bringing our inner feminine and masculine into perfect balance.

Now let's see what a disciplined practice of "The Inward Journey" could look like for you.

Chapter 9
"The Way"

I strongly suspect that many of you regularly practice some form of spiritual life, or at least enjoy reading spiritual material from time to time. Maybe you follow some kind of meditation or yogic practice. Regardless of what or how you do it, be it daily, weekly, monthly, or just sporadically, any and all of it is honoring "The Way," the "Inward Journey," in the form of learning how to sit in the absolute presence of our divine reality, listening within for what Life has to say to us.

We can witness or hear this inner authority in numerous ways: in focused meditation or while lovingly and fully engaged in life from moment to moment. If you have difficulty going within, you may find the suggested meditation in **Chapter 11** helpful.

The Three Questions method puts you in intimate contact with your inner authority, your innate wholeness, so you can listen to your highest good and release the fear or anxiety of not already having what you so deeply desire. The only difficulty is that we usually don't take the time or otherwise develop the skills and attitudes in order to listen intently from the depths of our heart.

This form of prayer helps you understand that it is *you* who *is* prayer, and that you only need to express your highest good. Until you develop the skill of listening moment to moment for the answer to what you truly are, this method can be a supporting bridge for you. If you practice it faithfully, you will develop the abilities and skills necessary for carrying you through life without any intermediary process. Eventually, you will simply have replaced old habits of prayer with the only one that is necessary: listening inwardly, as your inner authority provides the truth for you in all instances.

When we tune into the essence of prayer and live it moment by moment, the very need for it disappears. We begin to live in divine order, free from fear or anxiety of any kind.

This particular form of going within prayer life was taught to me years ago by an Episcopalian lay teacher, Jane Wolfe, and has been highly effective in revealing the secrets of what life is really about, for me but also for a host of others who have developed it as their spiritual discipline and practice.

Years ago, I taught this method among other presentations throughout Arkansas, Pennsylvania, Ohio, and New York. The emphasis was on establishing a discipline of "showing up" each day, taking ourselves to the place into which only Truth can be heard. The following testimonials give you a brief but clear idea of the impact of this process on two of the participants:

The first is from "Beth J.":

> "I really dug deep and felt the Spirit within me. During our

class I was unable to write anything, but the next morning, phew! The next morning my writings were amazing to me. I asked if I could read them in church that day, interestingly enough, there were no other messages from anyone else. That's quite unusual for our group.

"I have been writing daily. However, some days I am interrupted by one of my children, or I am unable to write. But I show up anyway. This amazing process of going inward has allowed me to open up a part of myself that I wasn't sure was going to open completely. This has been a real turning point for me and I am looking at a great many things very differently than I ever have."

Here's an example from "Beth J." of what came out of one of these spiritual moments:

Listen to your own song, beautiful. (I somehow got the message to turn on the song Imagine by Lennon.)

Unscramble the words and you
will know peace of mind.
Inner peace will come in time,
as long as you allow it to flow
in tune with your body and nature.
Open your eyes and look around.
Pay attention to nature and what you see. Make that connection, that deep, deep connection and you will know Me.

Remember who you are.
Look in the mirror and know you are perfection.
You are Me.
See Me.
See You.
See Us Together,
connected as One."

Here's another testimony, this one from "Kaye W." It was sent to me in a recent note, some six years after Kaye participated in my session:

> "As a side note, I still communicate with my Higher Self with my laptop. It's taken on more of a conversation kind of tone now. However I remain absolutely amazed at the insight and wisdom and guidance and love I am given. Several people have asked me recently if I am seeing "a professional" to help me deal with all the changes that are going on in my life. The answer is no, but I realized that's what I get from these conversations with my Higher Self, although I didn't think of it that way before. It's very hard to convey to people just how specific these messages that I receive are, how full of divine love and guidance. How could a counselor possibly compare? It would

take years for someone else to know me that well. And yet I sometimes still go into doubt, the ego takes over at times, and I work with that, too. I am often given guidance about my future that really seems, sometimes, way too good to be true. And even though I am beginning to see some of it manifesting already, there are definitely times when the ego loves to jump in and get me to fall back into fear. I wonder if you have experienced anything similar? (Do I hear laughter?)

All of this to say, AGAIN, how grateful I am for gaining this incredible tool, through which, in spite of my moments of doubt, I feel *so* awed by the changes in my life since this process began. Yes, there is loss and grief, but there is also so much joy, such a higher quality of love, such beautiful moments of being in the now."

And from one of Kaye's special moments:

> "Kaye, I am saying to your heart how very much I love you. I love you. I love you. I love you. I love you. I love you. I love you. I love you. Are you hearing me? Do you feel me? I will keep saying it over and over until you feel it in every fiber of your being, in every cell of your body. I love you. Do not be afraid. Do not fear. Your life is divinely guided. You are never alone. You are here to shine. Let yourself shine. Let yourself shine. Let yourself shine. Let yourself shine."

To add to this amazing testimony, Kaye W. just recently wrote me asking for some clarification, as she found someone else who wanted to learn the process and she wanted to assist her. On it goes…

It's now time for you to let *your own real voice* ring true to and for you.

YOU GOT THIS! Fear not. Ask.
Listen. Trust.

Chapter 10
The Three Questions

What follows is a very specific means of becoming more fully aware of your inner guidance. Try it; you'll like it! Have the courage to let go of any pre-conceived opinions and beliefs about finding spiritual guidance within.

In this inward journey, each of the following three questions begins with "Lord." Why "Lord"?

In spiritual terms, "Lord" is merely a contraction for Law of Order—and not some external God or other idol we call Lord and to whom we pray. Simply put, the Law of Order suggests that it is our own inner Voice we long to hear and follow. Hence, L'ord.

The Law of Order works simply to bring into life the particular connection we're exercising. If we're relying on outer authority and honoring ego consciousness, the Law of Order produces chaos, fear, lack, feelings of endless struggle, and lack of purpose. On the other hand, if we're honoring our inner Voice, peace, love, and joy express themselves continuously as our way in the world.

However, if the leap from believing in some kind of god to practicing the idea of L'ord is too much for you right now, don't despair. It's not what you call the still, small Voice that's important. What's important is that you're learning to listen inwardly to spiritual certainty, guidance that you can trust with all you are—and to demonstrate it with committed enthusiasm.

"The Inward Journey" is about empowering you and your divine essence, not about reinforcing separation from what you really are. It is not about seeking power in some external source, but about empowering you to be *all you already are: the immensity of your Being, your God-self, the highest version of you.*

So let's begin with this. First, simply sit with pen and paper, an audio recorder, or turn to your word processor, whichever feels most natural for you to record what comes to you. Just placing my fingers on the keyboard of the computer works best for me, but please do what is most natural for you.

Then, ask the three questions just as listed below, and follow the same process each time:

First, write down each question, one at a time.

If you're writing on paper, try placing the point of your pen or pencil on it, as if nudging it to start writing, and let it take you where it will. A similar feeling might come to you if you're using your word processor—placing your fingers lightly on the keyboard might just spark that first outpouring of messages.

Just sit and listen for the answer. Do NOT think. Just listen. This is not an ego exercise. It's a spiritual one. Ego deals with thinking we need to control everything. Being spiritual is about listening, *really* listening to our inner Voice. And that requires us to get out of our own way.

What normally happens is something often called "automatic writing". What we call it doesn't matter. What does matter is that we simply *allow* it.

You can't "think it" into being, so don't try. Don't judge it. Don't correct as you go along. Just transcribe the message that comes.

You will *know* when the answer from within is complete: it will simply feel like it *is* complete.

> ### 1. What, (insert your descriptor), are you saying to my heart?

Write down the question.
Wait.
Transcribe.
Give gratitude.

So you posed the question. And you waited. What happened?

If you didn't "receive" any message, that is perfectly fine. This is more about building a disciplined approach to listening inwardly than needing an answer the first few times you give yourself to the process. But if you stick to it, over time it does reap immense inner rewards, so keep on showing up.

If you find it difficult to open yourself up to this process, try focusing on the meditation in the next chapter. Give it a try—or come up with your own way of priming the pump of Truth to flow freely, fearlessly. Whatever it is that prompts you to go into your heart instead of your head, use it to get out of your own way.

Now, give thanks for this first answer and go on to the next question.

2. How, (   ), am I to respond to this?

Again, write down this question, and simply wait for the answer. Don't think about the answer. Just connect within and write down what you hear. The way this feels is that it's the answer writing itself for you when you are simply letting it happen, instead of trying to make it happen.

If there's a struggle, it means you're trying to *make* it happen instead of letting it have its way with you. And —that what you obtain will more than likely be coming from ego consciousness.

Give thanks to your inner Voice when the second question has been completed—or once you feel enough time has passed—and go on to the third.

> *3. What, (   ), do you particularly want me to remember?*

Once again, be fully present within, knowing that this relationship with your self provides the foundation for living spiritually. When you have finished all three questions, you might want to return to them, assimilating the answers into every fiber of your being.

Sometimes I type errors or use a word that doesn't sound like it was intended to be, so I correct these. But I do not change the intent or content of the answer. This would be an ego-driven act—a stubborn demand to substitute my answer for the Truth of my being. We do this most of the time already. But when you are listening for your inner guidance, it's time to change that habit.

Trust that this process will teach you to listen within for what is *really* best for you, spoken as your inner Truth, the voice of your wisdom. It replaces the habit of fulfilling the ego's demands for power and control.

In each instance of this loving communion with divine consciousness, profound insights occur. Fear releases. Enlightenment shows the way. For me, real answers are the ones that are best for me. Your answers will be what works best for you.

When I listen and let the messages of my inner Voice come to me, my behavior (or "demonstration," which I define as the outward expression of what I hear inwardly) is filled with integrity. Indeed, these messages are a perfect match of what is right *within* for me to what I express *outside* of me. In other words, I am loving and respecting myself and my neighbor in the purest form and with internal integrity intact.

When you feel fully infused with this inner joy and peace of mind, know this grace-filled feeling to be a sure sign that your inner feminine and masculine are working in tandem, equal in every way, balanced.

Living true to ourselves gives integrity to the love we share with others. Otherwise, we're extending a false sense of ourselves out into the Universe. How could extending a false sense of self into the world possibly be an expression of love?

Chapter 11
A Meditation to Start the "Inward Journey"

If you're having difficulty finding the time or mind space each day to initiate the practice of "The Way," try meditating on the following poem (or something like it)—and you might find that it relaxes and inspires you to ask the three questions with an open heart and mind.

Life

come, sit with me
let yourself simply be
plunge, if you will, to the depths of
your grief
loosen the slipknot on your weary
body and ravaged soul
freeing your burdens
your anger, your pain
whatever it is that discomforts you
whatever it is you feel

come, sit with me
open to the joy that is you
letting laughter's release unfold your

Truth
allow yourself to bask in my love for
you
healing your mind, your body, your
soul
bathe in the Light of transformation
knowing all you have to be is you
that I'm always here for you

come, sit with me
travel with me through the universe
be open in your silence
mindless in your solitude
resting your thoughts and feelings
here beside me
fully present in this art of
relationship
and you will come to know
yet again
that we are One

come, sit with me
no matter what the condition or
circumstance
no matter what our past
it is safe now.
in Eternal Friendship
this presence is all that matters

all we must do
is Be what we both
really are
divine
and these precious moments become
our Truth
authentic love our bond.

Why might this "way" of praying,
this inward journey, be thought of as
contrary to the usual forms of prayer
we've been taught? It turns the way
most people pray—and how they're
taught to pray—on its head, to living
from the inside out, rather than from
outer need perceived through our ego.
The latter, in fact, merely
spiritualizes ego consciousness,
rather than simply living spiritually.

This is the difference between
outwardly lived Christianity
normally ensconced in outer
authority, and the "The Inward
Journey" Jesus and other sages have
implored us to use. Now you know
the difference. And it will surely
make a difference in your life!

After all, if intuition or wisdom have never let you down, why would you follow some external authority? Why would you not think there are other *not?* choices? Indeed, follow the only way in which you find resonance with enthusiasm for life. It's the only life really worth being.

Congratulations! You have just taken a critical step on the road to mastering continuous prayer. Practice it regularly, diligently, adhering only to what you receive within. The inner Voice you hear and follow defines what you are, both as your character and your only true identity.

Chapter 12
Your Post-test

Now is the time to hear what you really are, which goes beyond what we normally accept—or are taught to accept—about ourselves. Take in the words below with the same spiritual intensity that guides you during your practice of "The Way."

These words are from the song *In His Eyes* (lyrics by Mindy Jostyn and Jacob Brackman). I've adapted the lyrics to provide the deepest meaning: the Truth about *you*. I can tell you the Truth about you; or you can hear the Truth about you inwardly. But in order for you to become fully aware of what you are, listening for the authentic resonance of these lyrics in your heart of hearts will validate your spiritual identity for you.

Be sure to take this Truth about you to heart:

In my eyes, I am a fire that never goes out, a light at the top of the hill.

In my eyes I am a poet, a painter, a prophet, with a mission of love to fulfill.

Outside there's a world so enchantingly strange, a maze of illusion and lies.

But there's never a story that ever could change the glory of me in my eyes.

In my eyes I am a radiant vision of beauty, a gemstone cut one of a kind.

I am as fine as a diamond, deep as a ruby, rare as jade in my mind.

No need to believe all I have been told, no need to live in disguise.

I am brighter than silver, purer than gold, a pearl beyond price in my eyes.

I see only goodness. My vision is true. And nothing can change the perfection of me in my eyes.

In my eyes I am a fire that never goes out, a light on top of the hill.

I am a rose in the forest, a prelude from Bach, a triumph of heaven's skill.

Outside there's a world that keeps breaking my heart, and tearing my dreams down to size.

But guiding me homeward, piercing the dark—is the love light that shines in my eyes.

Now and forever that light never dies. I am dearly beloved in my eyes.

Amen, I say to this. So be it—be *you*! May only blessings fill your life.

Chapter 13
Now What?

So what comes next? Nothing earth-shattering. Simply continue this leg of your journey in a similar fashion. One day, things may shift even further for you. You might discover that you don't need to ask the three questions at all, and that answers to questions you haven't even asked yet naturally come clearly to you.

Don't ruin the natural flow you've experienced thus far by thinking there's something else you "must" do. Simply let life come to you as you continue to open yourself to the beauty that abounds, starting within. It is those inner images and sensations that will most assuredly etch themselves indelibly on all levels of your being.

Having said that, if you are at all like I am, you'll probably say something like, "Gee, I sure wish I knew of this process long ago." So might it not be a good idea to share this simple process with others?

Actually, you probably won't even need to broach the topic with others at all. Merely from the changes in your demeanor, your uplifting attitude toward life, and your renewed energy and brilliant glow, you'll likely be asked about what's going on in your life. Don't be afraid to share. Remember that it's your duty only to deliver when asked. What anyone else does with what you tell them is up to them.

Here's an alternative for you. Once you're comfortable that this process is working for you, I invite you to take some time to simply describe how working through the Three Questions has been helpful to you. Just a few paragraphs will do, including an example.

If your experiences do make it into what could become a sequel to this book, you may well inspire others to follow a similar practice for living their purpose, their daily calling. And so I warmly invite you to send your offering to me at: creationspirit@gmail.com. There is, of course, no obligation.

Ask. Listen. Trust.

ACKNOWLEDGMENTS

I gratefully acknowledge the Spirit from which this creative expression comes. I enthusiastically and freely let Spirit flow through and from me, unrestrained by my ego. I did not try to fit it into a specific structure or to meet the needs of a specific readership. Thus I dedicate this book to the Highest Self that I am—and which we all are—and to freedom from fear, which prevents the immensity of our being from flowing with spiritual purpose.

My profound gratitude to Jane Wolfe for teaching me to go inward so I can hear the Word and express it into the Universe—and in turn inspire others and empower them to liberate and harness the immensity of their spiritual being as their day-to-day guide for living spiritually. I have integrated what Jane taught me into the process I describe in this book.

I greatly appreciate the endorsements from John Greer, Jenny Wagget, James C. Wilhelm and Annie Woods, friends and fellow authors who inspire and empower others with their own ideas and brilliant writing.

Gratitude, also, to Birgitte Rasine for her extraordinary edit on the text and her many other creative suggestions. I commend her most highly: birgitterasine.com.

Thanks goes to Beth J. and Kaye W., who so profoundly have demonstrated how practicing The Three Questions changed their everyday lives.

A very special thanks to the talented artist, Janalee Robison, who graciously granted permission to use one of her paintings for the front cover of this book. I express my heartfelt thanks to my youngest son, Todd Young, who encouraged me to bring The Three Questions into the universe as spiritual guidance for others.

To one and all, including you, the reader: THANK YOU, in the fullness of my heart!

Jim Young

About the Author

Dr. James (Jim) H. Young has served with distinction as a teacher, a distinguished professor of higher education and in a variety of leadership positions, including President (emeritus) of State University of New York at Potsdam and Chancellor (emeritus) of the University of Arkansas at Little Rock.

Jim is an internationally published award-winning spiritual author, poet and photographer, who reframes the spiritual perception of life in all aspects of his life's calling. A ministerial graduate of the Pecos Benedictine Monastery's Ecumenical School for Spiritual Directors and the Minister (emeritus) of the Creative Life Church in Hot Springs, AR, Jim is also co-founder of the Arkansas Metaphysical Society in Eureka Springs, and The Aristotle Group in Hot Springs.

In addition, he is an inspirational teacher who takes participants to the threshold of their own truth. To arrange presentations, workshops, and/or to join Jim's blog and (future) radio program, contact him as follows:

Web site/blog:
www.creationspirit.net
Email: creationspirit@gmail.com

BOOKS BY JIM YOUNG

(For descriptions:
www.creationspirit.net or
Amazon.com)

Perfect—Just Like You
The Three Questions
Aware in a World Asleep (O-Books)
Priceless Pearls for Misguided
Seekers
The Invitation
Living an Extraordinary Life in an
Ordinary Reality (O-Books)
2013! The Beginning is Here (O-
Books)
Letters Left Behind
Defrocking the Gospel of Thomas
God's Pocket Dictionary
As if from God
On Making Love; Spiritual
Testimony to the Gift Life Is

Surrender

What If...? Changing Your Life to
Fit Your Truth

Only Mind Matters: Emerging From
the Waters of Symbolic Meaning

Keys to the Door of Truth

A Labor of Love: Weaving Your
Own Virgin Birth on the Loom of
Life

The Creation Spirit: Expressing Your
Divinity in Everyday Life

Janalee Robison, whose painting is featured on the cover (by permission of the artist):

Janalee Robison's work utilizes the female narrative to explore personal and interpersonal relationships, spiritual and philosophical themes, and our earthly and spiritual journey and experiences. Janalee was born and raised in Topeka, Kansas. At a young age, she found a love of doodling and creating with various art mediums. This love coupled with a vivid imagination lead to a natural gravitation towards the visual arts. Janalee earned a Bachelor's Degree in Fine Art at the University of Kansas, with an emphasis in Printmaking. Janalee now resides in Eureka Springs, AR with her husband, Edward, and son, Ethan, were she creates art out of her home studio. Janalee also co-owns the Sacred Earth Gallery where original paintings, drawings, and prints of her

work can be purchased. Visit the
artist's website:
www.janaleerobison.com

Fr. Richard Rohr's prayer comes from Psalm 46:10 of the Hebrew Scriptures: "Be still and know that I am God." Use this prayer to draw yourself and others into a contemplative frame of mind.

Be still and know that I am God.
Be still and know that I am.
Be still and know.
Be still.
Be.

Made in the USA
Middletown, DE
30 October 2016